Explore the Universe
ALIEN PLANETS

WORLD
BOOK

a Scott Fetzer company
Chicago
www.worldbookonline.com

World Book, Inc.
233 N. Michigan Avenue
Chicago, IL 60601
U.S.A.

For information about other World Book publications, visit our Web site at **http://www.worldbookonline.com** or call **1-800-WORLDBK (967-5325).**

For information about sales to schools and libraries, call **1-800-975-3250 (United States),** or **1-800-837-5365 (Canada).**

Library of Congress Cataloging-in-Publication data
Alien planets.
  p. cm. -- (Explore the universe)
  Summary: "An introduction to extrasolar planets, with information about their formation and characteristics. Includes diagrams, fun facts, a glossary, a resource list, and an index"-- Provided by publisher.
  Includes index.
  ISBN 978-0-7166-9551-6
  1. Extrasolar planets--Juvenile literature. I. World Book, Inc.
  QB820.A45 2010
  523.2'4--dc22

                    2009040186

ISBN 978-0-7166-9544-8 (set)
Printed in China by Leo Paper Products, Ltd.,
  Heshan, Guangdong
1st printing February 2010

Cover image:
A rocky planet and its moon orbit a distant star, far from the sun and solar system, in an artist's illustration. The search for extrasolar planets, particularly one like Earth, is one of the most exciting areas of astronomy today.

WORLD BOOK illustration by Matt Carrington

CONTENTS

If a word is printed in **bold letters that look like this,** that word's meaning is given in the glossary on pages 60-61.

INTRODUCTION

For thousands of years, people have wondered if we are alone in the universe. Are there other worlds? Are they inhabited? In 1992, scientists answered the first of these questions. After a number of earlier reports proved inaccurate, astronomers announced the first true discovery of a planet outside the solar system. By the end of 2009, more than 400 extrasolar planets had been identified. In fact, it seems that extrasolar planets are fairly common in our region of the Milky Way. Do any of these planets support life—either in one of the many forms found on Earth or in a form altogether different? Astronomers are still searching for the answer to that question.

Many of the newly discovered ▶ extrasolar planets appear very different from the planets in the solar system.

THE CENTRAL STAR

The central **star** in a **planetary system** is usually a glowing ball composed mainly of **hydrogen** and **helium**. It is the only object in a planetary system that gives off its own light. The light comes from **nuclear fusion** reactions in the **core** of the star. High pressure and high temperatures cause the *nuclei* (cores) of hydrogen to fuse, or join together. This kind of nuclear reaction creates one larger nucleus of helium and gives off the tremendous energy that makes the star glow.

ORBITING OBJECTS

A planetary system can have large and small objects that orbit the central star. The largest objects are **planets**. A planet is a rounded body that shines because it reflects light from the central star. Sometimes smaller bodies called moons orbit a planet.

Objects much smaller than a planet and more like rocks or hunks of metal can also orbit a star. In addition, clouds of gas and dust sometimes surround the central star in a planetary system.

Extrasolar planet HD 188553 Ab, viewed from an imaginary moon in an artist's illustration, is a gaseous planet slightly larger than Jupiter. Found in 2005, HD 188553 Ab closely circles a central star that is also orbited by two other stars. The planet, about 149 light-years from Earth, was the first to be discovered in a triple-star system.

A planetary system is a group of objects in space that is usually made up of a central star and one or more planets and other objects that orbit, or travel around, that star. The planetary system that includes the sun is called the solar system.

Close-in planet HD 188553 Ab (not shown) zips around its central star in only 3.3 days. The two other stars in the system take 25.7 years to orbit the central star. These stars also circle each other every 156 days.

WHAT IS IN THE
SOLAR SYSTEM?

THE PLANETS

Eight large **planets** orbit the sun. Astronomers divide them into two groups. They call the planets closest to the sun the inner, *terrestrial* (Earth-like) planets. The terrestrial planets—Mercury, Venus, Earth, and Mars—are made of rock and metal and have solid surfaces. The four outer planets—Jupiter, Saturn, Uranus, and Neptune—are called **gas giants**. They are much bigger than Earth and are made mainly of **hydrogen** and **helium**. They have thick atmospheres but do not have solid surfaces.

Far out toward the edge of the **solar system** are icy objects called Kuiper belt objects. Orbiting with these objects is a thin cloud of gas and dust called the interplanetary medium.

The solar system also contains **dwarf planets,** objects that are smaller than planets. Pluto, which orbits far from the sun, was once considered a planet. The International Astronomical Union, which names space objects, declared that Pluto is actually a dwarf planet.

ASTEROIDS, COMETS, AND METEOROIDS

Most **asteroids**, which are much smaller than planets, orbit in a region between Mars and Jupiter. Asteroids come in all kinds of irregular shapes. The largest

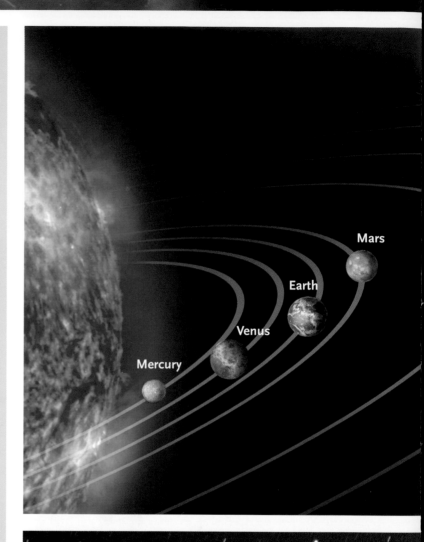

Discovered in 1996, the comet Hyakutake is one of thousands of comets and asteroids that orbit the sun. Some of these objects come from far beyond the orbit of Neptune. The long "tail" of a comet consists of dust, gas, and electrically charged particles that have been pushed away from the comet by solar radiation. These tails can be many thousands of miles long.

8 Explore the Universe

Neptune

Uranus

Saturn

Jupiter

The planetary system that includes Earth is called the solar system. It contains the sun, eight planets, several smaller planets called dwarf planets, more than 100 moons, and many millions of smaller objects.

known asteroid has a diameter of 605 miles (975 kilometers). The smallest known asteroids are about 20 feet (6 meters) in diameter.

Comets are balls of ice and rock. Some of them are too far out in space to be seen from Earth. Heat from the sun melts some of the ice, causing a cloud of gas and dust around the comet called a coma. When a comet streaks toward the inner solar system, it gives off a "tail" of dust.

Meteoroids are pieces of rock or metal like asteroids, but they are smaller than asteroids. Sometimes they fall to Earth. They make shining trails of hot gases called meteors as they fall through the atmosphere. Meteoroids that land on Earth are called meteorites.

HOW THE SOLAR SYSTEM FORMED

1 Astronomers believe that the solar system began as a rotating cloud of gas and dust, which they call the solar nebula. The cloud began to rotate faster and faster. As it rotated, gravity pulled the matter in the cloud into the shape of a disk.

2 The force of gravity continued pulling ▶ most of the matter in the disk toward the center. Eventually, this matter formed the sun. Deep in the sun, pressures and temperatures became so great that they triggered nuclear fusion reactions. The sun began to shine.

4 Eruptions of hot gases on the sun created the solar wind, a stream of electrically charged particles flowing out through the solar system. Astronomers think that the solar wind blew away most of the hydrogen, helium, and other lighter chemical elements around the inner planets. Far out, the solar wind was weaker, and the stronger gravity of the giant outer planets held on to more of the planets' hydrogen and helium. These outer planets kept most of their light elements and wound up with much more *mass* (amount of matter) than Earth.

▼

3 Other bits of dust in the disk collided and stuck together. These chunks kept growing because of continuing collisions. They formed asteroids. Some colliding asteroids formed larger bodies called planetesimals. Colliding planetesimals formed the planets.

Astronomers have long thought it likely that **planets** must orbit around some of the other 200 billion **stars** in our **galaxy,** the Milky Way. Planets that are outside of the **solar system** are called **extrasolar planets** or **exoplanets.**

Astronomers think that exoplanets form from a disk of matter orbiting a distant star. Such disks contain gas, dust, and pieces of rock or metal like the **asteroids** in the solar system. Astronomers believe this is how Earth and other planets in the solar system formed.

DID YOU KNOW?

The idea that other worlds like Earth exist in the heavens and that some of these worlds might support life dates back to the ancient Greeks.

Water and other potentially life-forming chemicals pool around rocks on an imaginary extrasolar planet, in an artist's illustration. The planet is shown orbiting a red dwarf, a star cooler than the sun.

WHAT IS A PLANET?

- Size: Should be at least 1,240 miles (2,000 kilometers) in diameter (Pluto's diameter is about 1,430 miles [2,300 kilometers]).

- Shape: Should be round, as the result of gravity shaping the material into a sphere.

- Orbit: Should orbit a star rather than another object in space and should have its own individual orbit.

- Mass: Should have a *mass* (amount of matter) that is greater than the combined mass of all other bodies in nearby orbits.

PLANETS AROUND A PULSAR

Alexander Wolszczan and Dale A. Frail found the first **exoplanets** while working at the Arecibo Observatory in Puerto Rico. The astronomers reported that at least two extrasolar planets were orbiting an unusual type of **star** called a **pulsar**. They later found a third exoplanet around the pulsar. Most pulsars give out powerful blasts of **radio waves** at regular intervals.

The first three exoplanets ever discovered orbit a *pulsar* (rapidly spinning star) called B1257+12 (upper left in an artist's illustration).

In 1992, a Polish astronomer and a Canadian astronomer reported finding the first exoplanets. They were using a telescope that detects radio waves from deep space.

The planets that orbit the pulsar B1257+12 are probably desolate places, unable to support life as we know it because of the intense radiation given off by the pulsar.

DID YOU KNOW?

If you could travel at the speed of light, it would take you more than 10 years to reach the nearest exoplanet.

PLANET AROUND A SUN-LIKE STAR

Swiss astronomers in 1995 announced they had discovered the first exoplanet orbiting a star like the sun. The exoplanet is similar in size to the **planet** Jupiter and orbits very close to the star, 51 Pegasi. The star is about 50 **light-years** from the **solar system.** A light-year is the distance light travels through space in one year, about 5.88 trillion miles (9.46 trillion kilometers).

HOW MANY EXTRASOLAR PLANETS HAVE BEEN DISCOVERED?

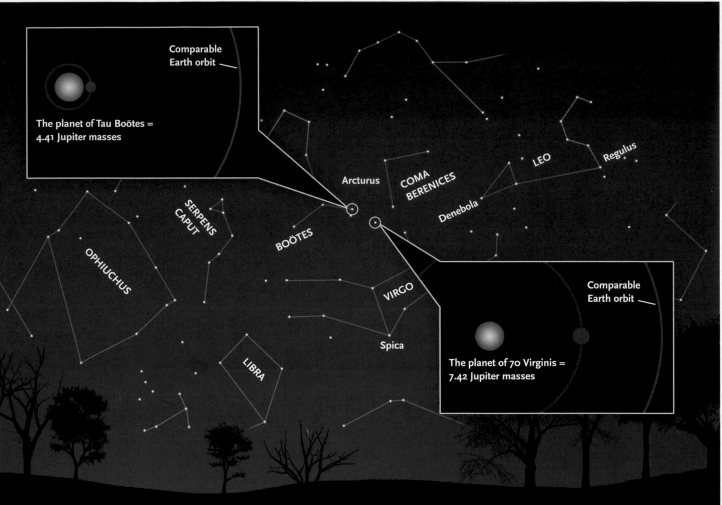

Comparable Earth orbit

The planet of Tau Boötes = 4.41 Jupiter masses

Arcturus

COMA BERENICES

LEO

Regulus

Denebola

SERPENS CAPUT

OPHIUCHUS

BOÖTES

VIRGO

Spica

LIBRA

Comparable Earth orbit

The planet of 70 Virginis = 7.42 Jupiter masses

Two stars with exoplanets are easily seen in Earth's night sky. Both of the stars, Tau Boötes and 70 Virginis, are located in the constellation Boötes. The planets orbit much closer to their central stars than Earth does to the sun (insets).

BETTER INSTRUMENTS

Astronomers believe that greatly improved instruments have helped in finding more **extrasolar planets.** More-sensitive detectors in **optical** telescopes are able to collect more visible light from distant **stars.** There have also been improvements in **spectrometers,** instruments used to analyze light from stars. More powerful computer software is better able to analyze information from distant stars about changes in their light and motion.

BIG PLANETS

Most of the exoplanets discovered so far are huge. They are many times the size of Earth. It is easier to detect huge planets than planets similar in size to Earth.

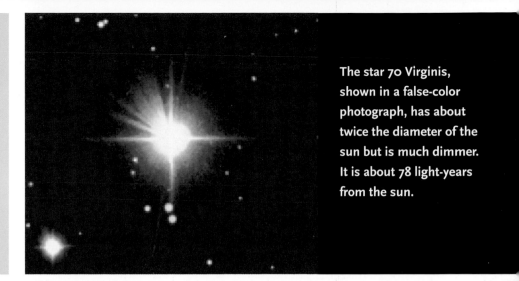

The star 70 Virginis, shown in a false-color photograph, has about twice the diameter of the sun but is much dimmer. It is about 78 light-years from the sun.

A ring of asteroids and other dusty debris orbits in the outer reaches of a planetary system like that around 70 Virginis, in an artist's drawing.

TINY FRACTION DISCOVERED

Just over 400 **planetary systems** had been discovered by the end of 2009. If there are billions of these systems, those discovered represent just a tiny fraction of the total out there. Only since the 1990's have astronomers had telescopes and other tools powerful enough to find planetary systems around distant **stars**.

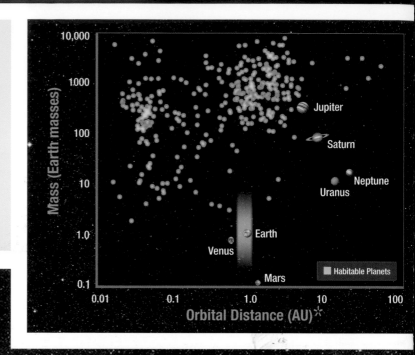

No one knows for sure how many planetary systems there are. Astronomers estimate that there could be billions of planetary systems around the 200 billion or so stars in our Milky Way Galaxy.

Most exoplanets found so far have a greater *mass* (amount of matter) than Earth. Many also follow an orbit that takes them much closer to their star than Earth's orbit around the sun.

* An AU (astronomical unit) is the average distance between Earth and the sun, 93 million miles (150 million kilometers).

DISCOVERY RATE INCREASES

Since the first **exoplanets** were discovered, new ones have been found at an increasing rate. Astronomers were finding an average of 25 new extrasolar planets each year in the early 2000's. About 30 different programs and institutions were devoted to looking for extrasolar planets. The discovery rate has increased as instruments have improved and more spacecraft carrying telescopes have been launched into orbit.

Billions of stars packed closely together light up the center of the Milky Way Galaxy. Many of these stars may be circled by planets.

HOW FAR AWAY ARE OTHER PLANETARY SYSTEMS?

DISTANCE IN LIGHT-YEARS

The distances in interstellar space are so vast that astronomers have special ways to measure them. One unit is the **light-year,** or the distance light travels in one year in a vacuum, 186,282 miles (299,792 kilometers) per second.

A light-year tells how many years it would take to reach a **star** while traveling at the speed of light. It also tells how long it takes for light from a star to reach Earth. The closest known **exoplanet** orbits the star Epsilon Eridani, which is 10.5 light-years away. The farthest known exoplanet is over 20,000 light-years away. Astronomers expect to discover more exoplanets in our region of the **galaxy.**

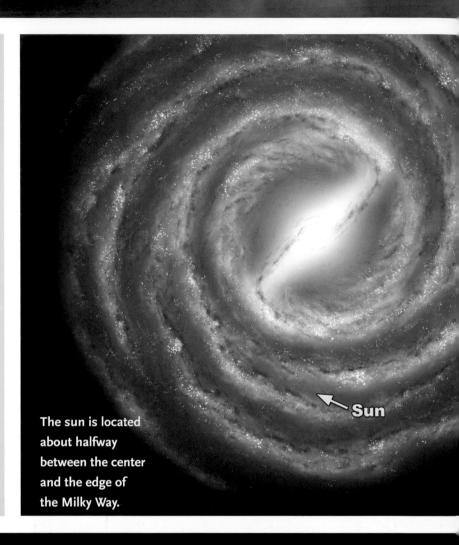

The sun is located about halfway between the center and the edge of the Milky Way.

Sun

How far away is the nearest exoplanet from Earth?

A radio signal...

...from the moon takes 1 second.

...from Mars takes 10 minutes.

...from the nearest extrasolar planet would take over 10 years.

The closest known extrasolar planet orbits the star Epsilon Eridani, which is 10.5 light-years away. The farthest known exoplanet is over 20,000 light-years away.

How far away have we searched for exoplanets?

If the entire solar system were the size of a United States quarter...

...our Milky Way Galaxy would be the size of the United States...

2,500 miles (4,000 kilometers)

...and the region where we have found the most new planets would only be the size of Manhattan Island in New York City.

ASTRONOMICAL UNITS

Another unit that astronomers use to measure distances in space is the **astronomical unit (AU).** An AU is the average distance between the sun and Earth, about 93 million miles (150 million kilometers). The AU is generally used for distances within **planetary systems** that are too large for miles or kilometers. The exoplanet 51 Pegasi b, which has about half the *mass* (amount of matter) of Jupiter, orbits only 0.05 AU from its central star, far closer than Mercury orbits the sun.

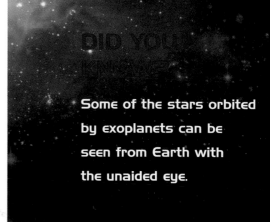

DID YOU KNOW?

Some of the stars orbited by exoplanets can be seen from Earth with the unaided eye.

DO MOST OTHER PLANETARY SYSTEMS HAVE STARS LIKE THE SUN?

An icy planet, five times the size of Earth, orbits a red dwarf star in an artist's depiction.

The sun is a glowing ball with a diameter of about 864,000 miles (1.4 million kilometers). It is made of a type of matter called **plasma.** Plasmas flow like a gas, carry an electric charge, conduct electricity, and are affected by magnetic fields.

BINARY STARS AND RED DWARFS

More than half of all **stars** the size of the sun are members of two-star systems called **binary stars.** The force of **gravity** holds the two stars together, and the two stars orbit around each other. Astronomers have found **exoplanets** in binary star systems.

A common type of star found at the center of **planetary systems** is called a **red dwarf.** These stars have less than half the **mass** (amount of matter) of the sun. They are small, relatively cool stars that glow with a dim, reddish light.

Most distant planetary systems may have stars that are very different from our sun.

NEUTRON STARS AND PULSARS

Exoplanets also orbit **neutron stars.** These objects are stars that have used up their nuclear fuel. A giant stellar explosion called a **supernova** blasts off the outer layers of the star. The central part of the star collapses to form a dense star.

Planetary systems also exist around **pulsars.** A pulsar is a neutron star that spins rapidly. Jets of **electromagnetic radiation** shoot from a pulsar's magnetic poles. Because a pulsar spins, from great distances it seems like a beam that is pulsing, or flashing, on and off.

Dust and pieces of rock from a shattered asteroid orbit a white dwarf in an artist's illustration. Astronomers have found exoplanets orbiting such stars, which are the cores of medium-sized stars that have used up all their fuel and thrown off their outer layers. The asteroid has crumbled because it came too close to the star and was broken up by the star's gravitational force.

WHAT OTHER PLANETARY SYSTEMS MIGHT BE LIKE

Other planetary systems have central stars very different from the sun. These stars include binary stars, red dwarfs, neutron stars, and pulsars. Many of the planets in these systems are huge and orbit very close to their central star.

Four of the five known planets in the 55 Cancri planetary system—e, b, c, and d—orbit their central star (below) in an artist's illustration. About 44 light-years from Earth, 55 Cancri is a yellow star about the same size as the sun but dimmer.

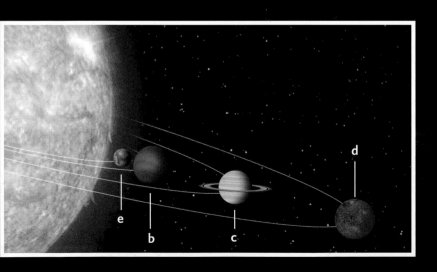

The planet 55 Cancri e circles its central star, 55 Cancri (left) in an artist's illustration. About the same mass as Neptune, 55 Cancri e orbits closer to its star than the planet Mercury orbits the sun.

   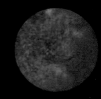

55 Cancri e

Mass   18 Earths
Orbit   3 days
Distance
   from star   0.04 AU*

55 Cancri b

Mass   0.84 Jupiters
Orbit   14.66 days
Distance
   from star   0.118 AU*

55 Cancri c

Mass   0.21 Jupiters
Orbit   44.28 days
Distance
   from star   0.24 AU*

55 Cancri d

Mass   4.05 Jupiters
Orbit   5,360 days
Distance
   from star   5.9 AU*

*An astronomical unit (AU) is the average distance between
Earth and the sun, 93 million miles (150 million kilometers).

IS IT HARD TO FIND EXTRASOLAR PLANETS?

FARAWAY STARS

Exoplanets are hard to find for several reasons. **Stars** that might have **planets** orbiting them are very far from Earth. One of the closest stars known to have a **planetary system** is more than 10 **light-years** away. It takes light from the star 10 years to reach telescopes on Earth.

DIM PLANETS

In addition, planets do not produce their own light. Planets are very dim because they shine from reflected light from their star. As a result, the light of a planet gets lost in the much brighter light from its star, just as a candle flame would be lost in the glare of a searchlight.

Trying to find an exoplanet by the light it reflects is like trying to spot a firefly sitting next to a spotlight. Stars may be billions of times brighter than their planets.

DID YOU KNOW?

Trying to find a planet around the closest star, Proxima Centauri, which is 4.2 billion light-years away, would be like someone in New York City trying to see a firefly near a spotlight in Los Angeles.

Several exoplanets have been found by scientists using the Hobby-Eberly Telescope in Texas, one of the world's largest *optical* telescopes (designed to gather visible light).

must search the sky with powerful telescopes. They must analyze the findings with sophisticated computers.

Most of the exoplanets discovered so far are very large. However, improved techniques and telescopes will allow us to find smaller, Earth-like planets.

This is what we have found.

This is what we are looking for.

HOW DO ASTRONOMERS LOOK FOR EXTRASOLAR PLANETS?

Astronomers usually do not try to take an actual photograph of an **extrasolar planet.** Instead, they look for telltale changes around **stars** that might indicate the presence of an exoplanet. These include changes in the the star's light caused by the movement or **gravity** of a **planet.**

When a planet passes in front of the star it orbits, it blocks some of the star's light. Sensitive instruments on or in orbit around Earth may be able to detect the change.

Planet   Star

Studying a star using telescopes that detect different forms of light may reveal the existence of an exoplanet. Outshone by the visible light of its star, an exoplanet appears almost invisible in an artist's illustration.

When viewed in the *infrared* (heat) portion of the electromagnetic spectrum, the planet appears much brighter.

Astronomers point telescopes at stars they think could have planets. They use powerful telescopes on Earth and orbiting telescopes in space.

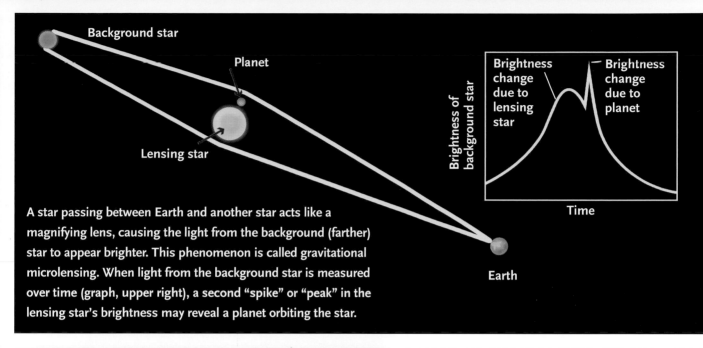

Background star

Planet

Lensing star

Earth

Brightness of background star

Brightness change due to lensing star

Brightness change due to planet

Time

A star passing between Earth and another star acts like a magnifying lens, causing the light from the background (farther) star to appear brighter. This phenomenon is called gravitational microlensing. When light from the background star is measured over time (graph, upper right), a second "spike" or "peak" in the lensing star's brightness may reveal a planet orbiting the star.

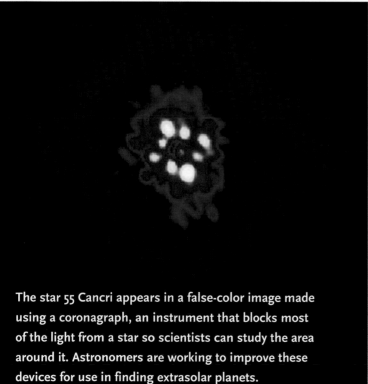

The star 55 Cancri appears in a false-color image made using a coronagraph, an instrument that blocks most of the light from a star so scientists can study the area around it. Astronomers are working to improve these devices for use in finding extrasolar planets.

WOBBLING STARS

Because of gravity, even a small planet tugs on the star it orbits. The planet's gravity makes the star wobble slightly. This wobble causes changes in the pulses of **visible light, radio waves,** or other **electromagnetic radiation** coming from the star. It causes changes in the position of a normal star in the sky.

CHANGES IN LIGHT WAVES

A star's wobble also creates changes in the **wavelengths** of light coming from the star. The wavelengths become shorter and then longer than normal as the star moves toward and away from the telescope pointed at it. These changes are called the **Doppler effect.**

THE TRANSITING METHOD FOR FINDING EXOPLANETS

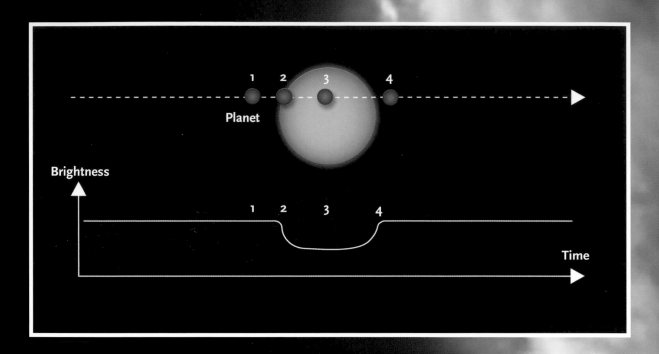

The brightness of a star can be dimmed by a planet passing in front of the star. This is called a *transit*. Before the planet begins to transit the star (1), the star is at its brightest. The light dims slightly as the planet begins to pass before it (2). When the planet passes directly in front of the star, it blocks more of the light (3). After the transit (4), the star's brightness returns to normal.

In 2006, the Hubble Space Telescope observed a section of the Milky Way Galaxy close to its center. During this observation, the telescope noticed 16 possible exoplanets. The astronomers used the transit method to spot these possible planets. One of the objects may be a planet larger than Jupiter that orbits close to its star, shown in an artist's depiction.

DOPPLER EFFECT IN SOUND

We can hear the **Doppler effect** in a train's whistle as the train approaches and then rushes past. When the train is approaching, the sound waves get compressed or pushed closer together. The sound has a high pitch. When the train passes and moves into the distance, the sound waves get stretched farther apart. The sound has a low pitch. A car's motor can produce the same effect as it passes a person standing still.

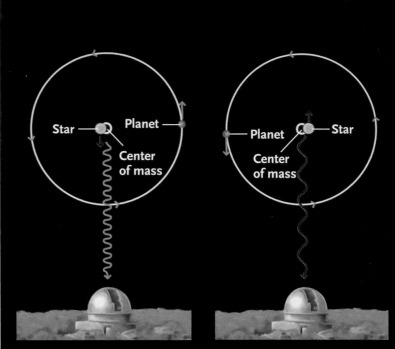

The light from a star can hold clues to the presence of a planet. Planets do not actually orbit their stars. Instead, both the star and planet orbit a common center of gravity. The star and planet are always on opposite sides of this center of mass. If the light from a star shifts regularly between shorter (bluer) and longer (redder) wavelengths, it indicates that a star must be alternately moving toward Earth (above left) and away from Earth (above right). This wobble may be caused by the gravitational force of the planet.

Sound waves from an approaching train are compressed, causing them to sound high-pitched to a person on the platform. As the train passes the person, the sound waves are stretched and so have a lower pitch. This is called the Doppler effect.

DOPPLER EFFECT IN LIGHT

Light waves also change with motion. Blue light has a shorter **wavelength.** Red light has a longer wavelength. When an object such as a **star** is moving toward Earth, the light waves get compressed, or shifted to the blue end of the **spectrum**. When the star is moving away from

The exoplanet Tau Boötes b orbits so close to its star that it is probably one of the hottest exoplanets known. The planet was one of the first discovered by using a computer analysis of its light.

Earth, the light gets stretched toward the red end of the spectrum. When astronomers see **blueshift** and **redshift** in the light from a star, they may conclude that the changes are caused by a planet's **gravity** tugging on the star.

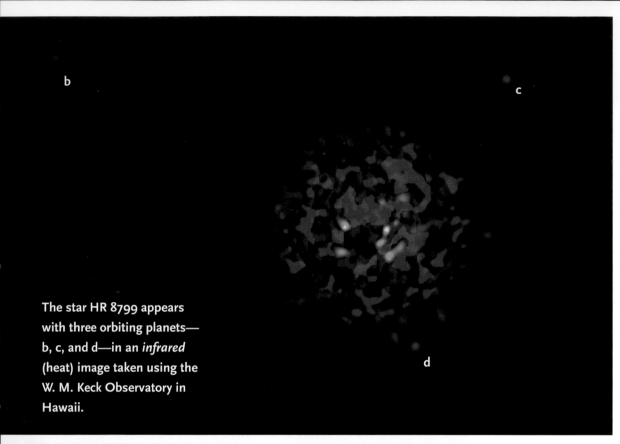

b

c

d

The star HR 8799 appears with three orbiting planets—b, c, and d—in an *infrared* (heat) image taken using the W. M. Keck Observatory in Hawaii.

Planet HR 8799 b, shown in an artist's illustration, is slightly larger than Jupiter but has about seven times as much *mass* (amount of matter).

In 2008, scientists published the first direct images of **extrasolar planets.** One image showed three **planets** orbiting a **star** called HR 8799. This star, in the **constellation** Pegasus, is 130 **light-years** from the **solar system.**

Astronomers also captured an image of a planet around a second star,

Most exoplanets have been discovered indirectly. In 2008, however, astronomers announced they had produced the first direct images of extrasolar planets.

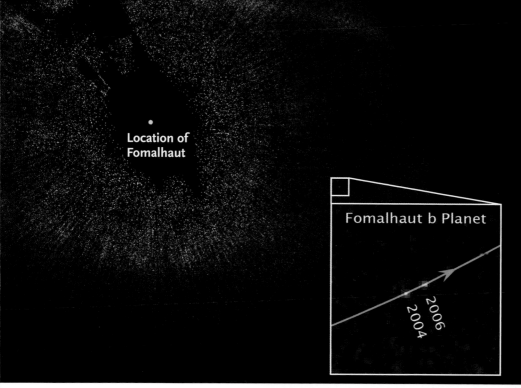

Location of Fomalhaut

Fomalhaut b Planet

2006
2004

A newly discovered exoplanet, Fomalhaut b, appears in two positions in its orbit around its star, Fomalhaut, in a combined image (inset left). The image was made by a camera on the Hubble Space Telescope that detected the infrared radiation emitted by the planet. The planet appears to orbit about 1.8 billion miles (2.9 billion kilometers) inside the huge disk of material that surrounds Fomalhaut (left).

Fomalhaut, in the constellation Piscis Austrinus. Fomalhaut is 25 light-years away.

Both stars are ringed by disks of gas and dust. Astronomers believe that the **exoplanets** formed from matter in these rings in the same way that the planets formed in the solar system.

The planet orbiting Fomalhaut, shown in an artist's illustration, ay be surrounded by a Saturn-like ring of material. The planet has about three times as much mass as Jupiter and orbits about 23 times as far from its star as Jupiter orbits from the sun.

Most of the **exoplanets** found so far are huge balls of gas. They do not have a solid surface as Earth does. Most of them orbit closer to their central **star** than Mercury, the innermost **planet** in the **solar system**. A planet this close to its star would be many times hotter than Earth.

The exoplanet Gliese 581c may lie within the habitable zone of its central star. Scientists are unsure whether the planet, viewed from an undiscovered moon in an artist's illustration, actually has liquid water and an atmosphere of wispy clouds.

DID YOU KNOW?

An exoplanet in the habitable zone of a star like the sun would take about one year to complete an orbit.

GLIESE 581C

In 2007, the most Earth-like planet yet was discovered around a **red dwarf** star Gliese 581. This star is about 20 **light-years** away. Astronomers named the planet, Gliese 581c. This exoplanet appears to lie in the "Goldilocks zone," or **habitable zone**. This zone is at just the right distance from the central star to make the planet neither too cold nor too hot for liquid water to exist. Liquid water is necessary for life as we know it to survive.

Astronomers have many questions about Gliese 581c. Does it really contain water? Does it have a rocky surface? Or is the planet covered completely by oceans?

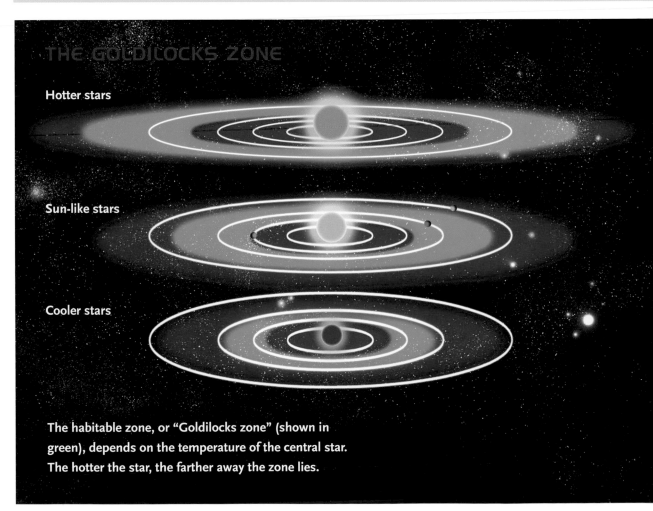

THE GOLDILOCKS ZONE

Hotter stars

Sun-like stars

Cooler stars

The habitable zone, or "Goldilocks zone" (shown in green), depends on the temperature of the central star. The hotter the star, the farther away the zone lies.

WHAT IS A SUPER-EARTH?

COLD SUPER-EARTH

A super-Earth can be up to 10 times the **mass** (amount of matter) of Earth. Most super-Earths are too cold to support life. Some astronomers think icy super-Earths form around **red dwarf stars** because of solar snowstorms. The red dwarf dims, causing the surrounding disk of gas and dust to cool. Gas changes to ice and, over millions of years, falls on the super-Earth, causing it to grow ever larger.

A super-Earth orbits a red dwarf star in an artist's image.

smaller than an exoplanet made of gases. Astronomers believe that super-Earths are made of rock and ice.

Some super-Earths may have satellites similar to Earth's moon. A large moon orbits close to a super-Earth circling a red dwarf in an illustration.

HOT SUPER-EARTH

In 2009, astronomers discovered the smallest **exoplanet** known. Called CoRoT-Exo-7b, it is less than twice the size of Earth. It orbits so close to its star that it completes one orbit in only about 20 hours on Earth. This super-Earth is made of rock, but it is too hot for life. Its surface temperature reaches 2,700 °F (1,500 °C) because the exoplanet orbits so close to its star.

WHAT IS A PULSAR PLANET?

A wide ring of debris surrounds pulsar 4U 0142+61 in an artist's illustration. The pulsar, discovered by NASA's Spitzer Space Telescope, exploded about 100,000 years ago, scattering dust and gas into space. Astronomers speculate that planets might develop from material in the ring. The pulsar is about 10 miles (16 kilometers) wide but has about 1 1/2 times as much *mass* (amount of matter) as the sun.

DID YOU KNOW?

The first exoplanets discovered were orbiting a pulsar. The first planetary system discovered had a pulsar as its central star.

A pulsar planet is a planet in orbit around a dense star called a pulsar.

The beams of intense radiation from a pulsar, shown in an artist's illustration, would blast any nearby planets, making life as we know it impossible.

Pulsars are rapidly rotating **neutron stars** that form when a large dying **star** explodes in a huge blast called a **supernova.** Pulsars give off regular bursts of **electromagnetic radiation.**

BEFORE THE SUPERNOVA

Astronomers have two main ideas about how pulsar **planets** form. They could form around the original star, the way planets in the **solar system** formed, and then somehow survive the supernova. Astronomers believe this is unlikely. The force of the explosion would destroy any existing planets or blow them out of that **planetary system.**

AFTER THE SUPERNOVA

It is more likely that a pulsar planet forms after a supernova. Some of the outer layers blown off the star may form a disk of gas and dust around the pulsar. Over time, **gravity** causes some of the matter to clump together into larger pieces that eventually form rocky planets.

Life on a pulsar planet is unlikely. **X rays** and other high-energy radiation coming from pulsars bombard the planets. Life as we know it could not exist in the presence of this lethal radiation.

WHAT EXTRASOLAR PLANETS MIGHT LOOK LIKE

No one has seen an extrasolar planet up close. So astronomers and artists use data from telescopes and other instruments to estimate what they look like. For example, they analyze light reflected by the planet for clues to chemicals that make up its atmosphere or surface.

The extrasolar planet HD 70642b, which is about twice as massive as Jupiter, dominates the sky above a hypothetical moon in an artist's illustration. The planet's orbit, which is about 3/5 the distance from its star as Jupiter is from the sun, suggests that smaller, possibly Earth-like planets might also be a part of this planetary system.

HD 209458b, shown orbiting its central star in an artist's illustration, is one of many hot Jupiters discovered in the Milky Way Galaxy. Such planets are at least as massive as Jupiter but orbit much closer to their central star. HD 209458b circles its star at a distance less than 1/5 of the distance between Mercury and the sun. The temperature on the surface of the planet is about 1,830 °F (1,000 °C), more than twice as hot as Mercury.

Gas giants are unlike terrestrial **planets,** which are rocky and have solid surfaces. Almost half of the **exoplanets** discovered so far are gas giants.

GAS GIANTS IN THE SOLAR SYSTEM

Four planets in the **solar system** are gas giants—Jupiter, Saturn, Uranus, and Neptune. Jupiter is the largest planet, with a diameter at its equator of about 88,800 miles (143,000 kilometers). Neptune, with a diameter at its equator of about 30,800 miles (49,500 kilometers), is the farthest planet from the sun. The gas giants are in the outer solar system. They are very cold. The temperature at the top of Jupiter's cloudy atmosphere is about –230 °F (–145 °C). The temperature at the top of Neptune's clouds is about –355 °F (–215 °C).

The gas giant Jupiter is the largest planet in the solar system. More than 1,300 Earths could fit inside Jupiter.

DID YOU KNOW?

Because they are made chiefly of gases, gas giants are much less dense than rocky planets like Earth. Saturn would actually float if it were placed in water.

A gas giant is a huge ball of gas many times larger than Earth. It does not have a solid surface, but it might have a core made of liquid or metal.

Swirling gases that create vivid patterns on the surface of Jupiter are captured in a composite photograph taken by the New Horizons probe.

HOT OR COLD BEGINNING

Some astronomers believe the gas giants began as huge balls of ice far out in the solar system. Over time, they attracted more matter in the form of gases. As the planets grew larger, their **gravity** pulled in more and more gases. Other astronomers think that these planets began as balls of gas. When they grew larger, their gravity drew in the solid matter that would form their cores.

The Great Red Spot (center) and the Little Red Spot (middle right) on Jupiter are believed to be long-lasting storms, similar in appearance to cyclones on Earth.

WHAT IS A HOT JUPITER?

HOW HOT JUPITERS FORMED

Because **hot Jupiters** orbit so close to their central **stars,** their temperatures are very high. Astronomers believe that hot Jupiters formed from gas and dust in the disk around the star. But these **planets** could not have formed close to their star, because there was not enough gas in the inner disk. Heat from the star would have driven off gases and water vapor from the disk, leaving only solid matter. Instead, these **gas giants** probably formed far out in their **planetary systems,** where gases were frozen into ice. Later, the hot Jupiters migrated in toward the central star, scientists theorize.

JUPITER

- Composed primarily of hydrogen and helium
- Orbit duration = 12 Earth years
- Cloud-top temperatures = -255 °F
- Radius = 1 Jupiter radius
- Mass = 1 Jupiter mass
- Average density = 1.33 g/cm³
- Moon, rings, magnetosphere = yes
- Distance from sun = 5 times Earth's distance from the sun

A hot Jupiter called HD 149026b, shown in an artist's illustration, is believed to be one of the hottest exoplanets known. The surface temperature is 3,700 °F (2,040 °C).

A hot Jupiter is an extrasolar planet that has about the same mass as Jupiter but orbits much closer to its central star than Jupiter does to the sun.

HOT JUPITER

- Composed primarily of hydrogen and helium
- Orbit duration = as short as 1.2 Earth days
- Cloud-top temperatures = 1,880 °F
- Radius = up to 1.3 Jupiter radius
- Mass = 0.2 to 2 Juplter masses
- Average density = as low as 0.3 g/cm^3
- Moon, rings, magnetosphere = unknown
- Distance to star = closer than the orbit of Mercury

A hot Jupiter known as SWEEPS-10 (upper right in an artist's illustration) speeds completely around its star in only about 10 hours. The planet orbits so close to the star that its atmosphere is likely being blown away by the star's solar wind.

A newly formed gas giant orbits a young sun-like star in an artist's illustration. Like the gas giants in the solar system, extrasolar gas giants may also have moons.

SIGNS OF WATER

In 2007, astronomers found a hot Jupiter that showed signs of containing liquid water. The planet, named HD 189733b, is in a planetary system about 63 **light-years** away. This hot Jupiter has temperatures in its atmosphere of about 1,300 °F (700 °C).

WHAT IS A HOT NEPTUNE?

Some hot Neptunes may be covered by a thick layer of hot ice—water that is forced to remain solid by the high pressure caused by the gravitational pull of the star, despite the planet's high surface temperature.

PUZZLING PLANETS

Hot Neptunes are much warmer than Neptune. One of the first known hot Neptunes was Gliese 436b, first observed in 2004. Its orbit is about 1,000 times as close to its **star** as Neptune's is to the sun. Gliese 436b goes around its star in little more

A hot Neptune is an extrasolar planet similar in size to Neptune. However, unlike Neptune, this type of exoplanet orbits close to its central star.

The exoplanet Gliese 436b, shown in an artist's illustration, is considered a "hot Neptune." The star this exoplanet orbits is only 40 percent the size of the sun and is much cooler. However, the planet orbits a mere 2.6 million miles (4.1 million kilometers) away, causing the surface of the planet to heat up to 698 °F (370 °C).

than 2 1/2 Earth days. Astronomers believe that hot Neptunes, like **hot Jupiters,** formed in the cold outer parts of a disk of gas and dust circling a star. The **planets** then migrated close in to the star, growing increasingly hotter.

Extrasolar hot Neptunes discovered so far are about twice the size of Earth with about 20 times the mass. Astronomers are unsure whether they are rocky planets like Earth or gaseous planets like Jupiter.

WHAT MAKES EARTH RIGHT FOR LIFE?

RIGHT TEMPERATURE

In its position around the sun, Earth is in the **habitable zone.** Its temperature is just right for life. It is cool enough to allow liquid water to form, and it is warm enough to prevent water from freezing. Water is needed for life as we know it.

Earth lies in the habitable zone, the region of a planetary system thought to be the best place for life to develop.

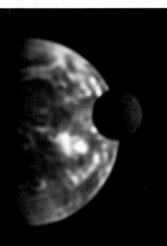

The moon passes across Earth in an image taken from 31 million miles (50 million kilometers) away by NASA probe Deep Impact. Scientists are using images from the probe to help them learn how an Earth-like planet outside the solar system might appear from a distance.

Of all the planets and moons in the solar system, Earth is the only one known to support life. Earth has a unique set of circumstances that make life as we know it possible.

RIGHT ATMOSPHERE

Earth's atmosphere also contains gases that help make life possible. The atmosphere contains just the right amount of so-called **greenhouse gases.** These gases include methane and carbon dioxide. Greenhouse gases prevent heat from the sun that reaches Earth from escaping into space. Like glass in a greenhouse, the gases help make Earth warm enough for life. Large amounts of greenhouse gases, however, would make Earth too hot to support life.

Earth has the right mix of gases in its atmosphere. It has oxygen, which animals must breathe and plants need to make food. When animals breathe out, they give off carbon dioxide. Plants give off oxygen.

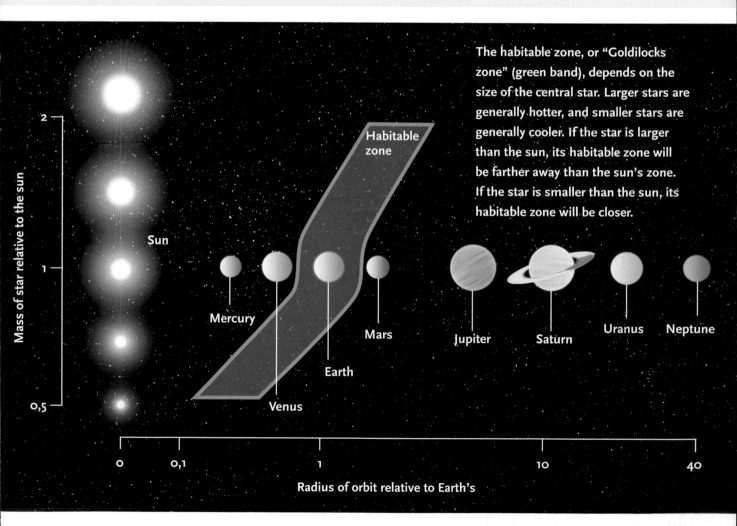

The habitable zone, or "Goldilocks zone" (green band), depends on the size of the central star. Larger stars are generally hotter, and smaller stars are generally cooler. If the star is larger than the sun, its habitable zone will be farther away than the sun's zone. If the star is smaller than the sun, its habitable zone will be closer.

Mass of star relative to the sun

Radius of orbit relative to Earth's

Hydrothermal vents in the ocean floor, called "hot smokers," provide nutrients for animals living around them. These animals, which include shrimp, crabs, fish, and giant tubeworms (inset), do not depend on the sun to provide the energy for life. Other forms of life on Earth have developed additional ways to survive without the sun as their source of energy.

EARTH-LIKE CONDITIONS REQUIRED

For life as we know it to exist on an **exoplanet**, the **planet** must be about the same temperature as Earth. Other factors, such as the size of the planet and a magnetic field around the planet, may also be necessary. Astronomers estimate that there could be about 100 billion Earth-like exoplanets in the Milky Way.

BLACK PLANTS

Astronomers and biologists are developing new ideas about what life on extrasolar planets could be like. For example, plants on an alien world might be black instead of green. A black plant would be able to absorb more light if its central **star** was a dim star, such as a **red dwarf**.

In order for an extrasolar planet to support life similar to that on Earth, it cannot be a gas giant. It must be a solid, rocky planet like Earth.

LIVING CRYSTALS

Life on Earth needs DNA molecules and proteins to reproduce and function. Space scientists, however, are studying the possibility of "weird life" on other worlds. They have found that when **plasma,** a gas-like form of matter that makes up the sun and other stars, comes in contact with dust in clouds, crystals form. In experiments on the International Space Station, plasma crystals formed the twisted ladder shape of DNA, divided to reproduce, and even seemed to evolve. Could alien life be based on plasma crystals?

A microbe found in Lake Vostok, a lake 2 miles (3 kilometers) below Antarctica's permanent ice cover survives without light, air, or warmth.

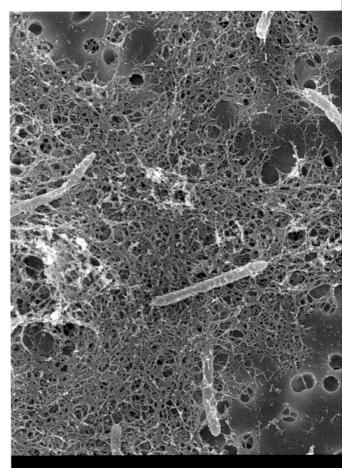

Bacteria found in a gold mine in South Africa flourish without energy from the sun. They get energy from the radioactive elements in the rocks around them.

BIG ENOUGH TO HOLD GASES

Planetary scientists have learned a great deal about how size affects atmospheres by studying the **planets** in the **solar system.** A planet must be large enough so that its **gravity** can attract and hold onto gases. When the eight planets in the solar system formed from matter in the solar **nebula**, their gravity drew in **hydrogen** and **helium.** All the planets were big enough to have atmospheres made up of these gases. Over time, the sun grew hotter, and its energy drove off the light hydrogen and helium gases around the four inner planets. Mercury, Venus, Earth, and Mars had no atmosphere at all.

Volcanoes on Earth and several other planets in the solar system are a source of the gases that help make up the atmosphere.

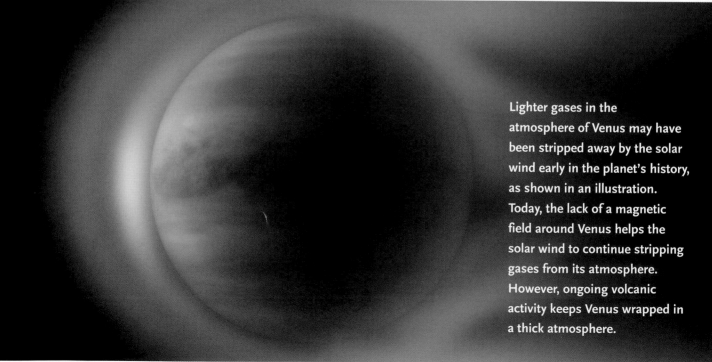

Lighter gases in the atmosphere of Venus may have been stripped away by the solar wind early in the planet's history, as shown in an illustration. Today, the lack of a magnetic field around Venus helps the solar wind to continue stripping gases from its atmosphere. However, ongoing volcanic activity keeps Venus wrapped in a thick atmosphere.

The chance of life developing on a planet depends on what kind of atmosphere it has. The type of atmosphere a planet has depends on its size and distance from its star.

POSITION IS IMPORTANT, TOO

Over time, secondary atmospheres formed on all four planets as volcanoes erupted. The eruptions released water vapor and carbon dioxide trapped in the rocks. Mercury was too small, with too little gravity to hold on to its secondary atmosphere. Venus is about the same size as Earth. It is so close to the sun, however, that its water vapor burned away, leaving only carbon dioxide.

Scientists believe Mars lost its secondary atmosphere for two main reasons. First, its volcanoes stopped erupting gases that would have resupplied its atmosphere. Second, its magnetic field disappeared, for various possible reasons. As a result, the flow of electrically charged particles from the sun stripped away the atmosphere. Mars is so far from the sun that without an atmosphere to warm its surface, its surface water froze to ice.

Mars had a much thicker atmosphere and may have had a strong magnetic field in the past. Some scientific evidence suggests that a meteor impact early in Mars's history may have disrupted this magnetic field. This allowed the gases to escape faster than Mars could replace them.

HOW WILL SCIENTISTS KNOW IF THERE IS LIFE ON AN EXTRASOLAR PLANET?

CLUES IN THE ATMOSPHERE

When they find an Earth-size **exoplanet,** scientists will analyze the **spectrum,** or rainbow of colors, in its light. Molecules of different chemicals absorb the colors, or bands of light, in telltale ways. First, scientists will look for signs of an atmosphere. They will try to determine what gases make up the atmosphere. They will also look for water molecules, signs of liquid water on the planet.

Scientists will compare the gases that make up an exoplanet's atmosphere to gases in Earth's ancient atmospheres. They have charted how Earth's atmosphere has evolved over millions of years. The atmosphere of early Earth contained no free oxygen. Our atmosphere evolved as simple life forms, such as bacteria, gave off oxygen that more complex life forms could use. After plant-like life evolved, **photosynthesis** released oxygen into the atmosphere as a waste product. An exoplanet's atmosphere might be evolving in similar ways.

Exoplanet HD 189733b, shown in an artist's drawing, has an atmosphere with methane and water, elements that may be signs of life.

many light-years away, scientists will look for clues in the light coming from these exoplanets.

SIGNS OF A BIOSIGNATURE

Then scientists will look for what they call a **biosignature.** A biosignature is a sign of life. On an exoplanet, it would be a gas in the atmosphere that could be produced by living things. A combination of carbon dioxide, oxygen, and water vapor could be a biosignature indicating that plant photosynthesis was going on. Methane gas could be a biosignature indicating the existence of bacteria and animal life. Ozone in the atmosphere could indicate the presence of algae and plants.

HOW A PLANET SUPPORTS LIFE

Plants and algae on Earth produce oxygen gas.

All life as we know it cannot function without liquid water.

Many living organisms on Earth produce methane gas.

ARE THERE NEW WAYS TO SEARCH FOR EXTRASOLAR PLANETS?

GROUND-BASED PLANET-HUNTING MISSIONS

Atop Hawaii's Mauna Kea, light from two telescopes was combined in the Keck Interferometer to create the most powerful virtual telescope on Earth. The light collected using **interferometry** looks as if it were collected by one giant telescope. Keck astronomers in the early 2000's began aiming the telescopes at stars that could have Earth-like **planets.** They hoped to take pictures of any planets they found.

Slated to join in the search for Earth-like planets is the Large Binocular Telescope Interferometer. These telescopes have two mirrors that act like gigantic binoculars. They were built in the Arizona desert.

SPACE-BASED PLANET-HUNTING MISSIONS

The first space-based mission dedicated solely to looking for Earth-like planets, the Kepler Mission, was launched in 2009. Kepler was designed to focus for 3 1/2 years on just one area of the Milky Way Galaxy. Its telescope was designed to examine this area for signs of planets passing in front of their stars. Keck and Kepler formed a team in 2009 using the power of both their instruments in the Earth-like planet search. Once Kepler detects what appears to be a planet, the Keck

The European Space Agency's COROT satellite, shown in an artist's illustration, was launched in 2006. It was the first spacecraft launched to look for rocky, Earth-like planets.

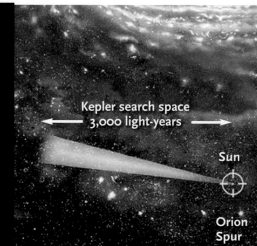

The Kepler Mission will search for rocky planets orbiting sun-like stars in a small section of the Milky Way Galaxy. The telescope will stare at about 100,000 stars for five years.

Kepler search space
3,000 light-years

Sun

Orion Spur

astronomers will use their telescopes to study the light coming from it.

The orbiting SIM Lite Astrometric Observatory was scheduled to follow up on the Kepler Mission findings. SIM Lite will use **optical** interferometry. Instruments on SIM Lite will measure with great precision the wobble of stars with suspected **exoplanets** in relation to other stars in the background. Using interferometry in space, astronomers will one day be able to take clear pictures of distant exoplanets.

FUTURE MISSIONS

The Terrestrial Planet Finder (TPF) project, under study by NASA scientists, aims to look for Earth-like planets in the **habitable zones** of distant **planetary systems.** The TPF missions will use various techniques to reduce the light from **stars** so scientists can measure the temperature, size, and orbit of any orbiting planets.

The Canadian Space Agency's MOST satellite, shown in an illustration, searches for extrasolar planets, among its other missions.

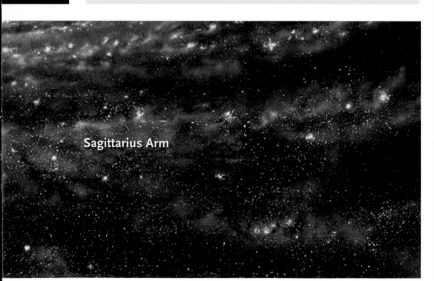

Sagittarius Arm

Launched in 2009, NASA's Kepler space telescope has a main mirror that is 4.6 feet (1.4 meters) in diameter.

GLOSSARY

Asteroid – A small, rocky body orbiting a star.

Astronomical unit (AU) – A unit of measure used to express distance within planetary systems. An AU is equal to the average distance between Earth and the sun, or about 93 million miles (150 million kilometers).

Binary stars – Stars that orbit each other.

Biosignature – Any chemical or electromagnetic sign of life. In astronomy, the detection of carbon dioxide, oxygen, and water vapor in a planet's atmosphere would be considered a biosignature.

Blueshift – A shift in light's wavelength toward shorter, blue wavelengths. Light from stars or other bodies approaching the Earth may show blueshift.

Comet – A small, icy body orbiting a star.

Core – The dense, hot center of a star.

Constellation – A group of stars that resembles a familiar shape in the sky. Astronomers have divided the night sky into 88 constellations, such as Orion (the Hunter).

Doppler effect – The change in wavelength of light or sound caused by the relative motion of the source and the observer.

Dwarf planet – A rocky body that is smaller than a true planet but larger than an asteroid.

Electromagnetic radiation – Any form of light, ranging from radio waves, to microwaves, to infrared light, to visible light, to ultraviolet light, to X rays, to gamma rays. Radio waves have the longest wavelength and lowest energy, and gamma rays have the shortest wavelength and highest energy.

Extrasolar planet (exoplanet) – Any planet in orbit around a star other than the sun.

Galaxy – A vast system of stars, gas, dust, and other matter held together in space by mutual gravitational pull.

Gas giant – A relatively large planet primarily made up of gas rather than rocky material.

Gravity – The force of attraction that acts between all objects because of their mass.

Greenhouse gas – Any gas that traps heat in a planet's atmosphere through the greenhouse effect. Carbon dioxide and methane are both examples of greenhouse gases.

Habitable zone – The area around a star in which a planet may contain liquid water. Exoplanets in habitable zones are thought to hold the best prospects for supporting life as we know it. Earth is in the habitable zone of the sun.

Helium – The second simplest chemical element. Helium is produced through the nuclear fusion of hydrogen.

Hot Jupiter – An exoplanet similar in size to Jupiter that orbits relatively close to its central star.

Hot Neptune – An exoplanet similar in size to Neptune that orbits relatively close to its central star.

Hydrogen – The simplest chemical element. Hydrogen is the most abundant substance in the universe. It fuels most stars.

Interferometry – A technique in astronomy whereby two or more telescopes are combined to act as one large telescope. Interferometry can be used to produce sharper images than an individual telescope could produce.

Mass – The amount of matter in an object.

Meteoroid — A piece of rock or metal similar to an asteroid but of smaller size. Meteoroids that strike the Earth's atmosphere and form glowing streaks are called meteors. Meteoroids that reach the surface of the Earth are called meteorites.

Nebula — A cloud of dust and gas in space.

Neutron star — A star that has collapsed into a small area with extremely high mass. Neutron stars form from the remains of massive stars that have exploded in supernovae.

Nuclear fusion — The combination of two or more atomic nuclei (cores) to form the nucleus of a heavier element. Nuclear fusion releases the energy that powers stars.

Optical — Of or relating to visible light. For example, optical telescopes gather and focus visible light.

Photosynthesis — The chemical process by which plants, algae, and other living things convert light energy from the sun into chemical energy such as sugar.

Planet — A large, round heavenly body that orbits a star.

Planetary system — A group of objects usually made up of a central star and one or more orbiting planets. The planetary system that includes the sun is called the solar system.

Plasma — A gas-like form of matter composed of electrically charged particles.

Pulsar — A neutron star that produces pulses of radio waves or other electromagnetic radiation at regular intervals.

Radio waves — The form of light with the longest wavelengths. Radio waves are invisible to the naked eye.

Red dwarf — A small, relatively cool star that glows with a dim, reddish light. Red dwarfs range in mass from about 1/12 to 1/2 the mass of the sun.

Redshift — A shift in light's wavelength toward longer, redder wavelengths.

Solar system — The planetary system that includes the sun and Earth.

Spectrometer — An astronomical instrument that divides light into a spectrum and records it for analysis.

Spectrum, spectra — Light divided into its different wavelengths. A spectrum may provide astronomers with information about a heavenly body's chemical composition, motion, and distance.

Star — A huge, shining ball in space that produces a tremendous amount of light and other forms of energy.

Supernova — An exploding star that can become billions of times as bright as the sun before gradually fading from view. A supernova occurs when a massive star uses up all its fuel.

Visible light — The form of light human beings can see with their eyes.

Wavelength — The distance between successive crests, or peaks, of a wave. Wavelength is used to distinguish among different forms of light.

X rays — A form of light with very short wavelengths. X rays are invisible to the unaided eye.

FOR MORE INFORMATION

WEB SITES

Catalog of Exoplanets

http://www.planetary.org

The Planetary Society's database of all known planets outside the solar system, with information about when each was discovered, its location, size, orbit, and central star.

The Extrasolar Planets Encyclopaedia

http://exoplanet.eu

Produced in Europe, this Web site's "Extrasolar Planets Global Searches" page tracks current and future projects and programs in outer-space research.

Planet Quest

http://planetquest.jpl.nasa.gov

NASA's Jet Propulsion Laboratory presents information on discoveries of extrasolar planets, with updates on the Kepler Space Telescope and other missions.

BOOKS

Extrasolar Planets

by Ron Miller (Twenty-first Century Books, 2002)

Infinite Worlds: An Illustrated Voyage to Planets Beyond Our Sun

by Ray Villard and Lynette R. Cook (University of California Press, 2005)

Life on Other Planets

by Rhonda Lucas Donald (Franklin Watts, 2003)

Outer Limits: The Future of Space Exploration

by Gary Miller (Gareth Stevens, 2009)

INDEX

ACKNOWLEDGMENTS

The publishers acknowledge the following sources for illustrations. Credits read from top to bottom, left to right, on their respective pages. All illustrations, maps, charts, and diagrams were prepared by the staff unless otherwise noted.

Cover:	WORLD BOOK illustration by Matt Carrington
1	NASA/JPL-Caltech
4-5	© David A. Hardy, astroart.org/STFC
6-7	NASA/JPL-Caltech
8-9	NASA/JPL; © Frank Zullo, Photo Researchers
10-11	WORLD BOOK illustrations by Matt Carrington
12-13	NASA/JPL-Caltech
14-15	NASA/JPL-Caltech; © Ron Miller
16-17	WORLD BOOK illustration by Matt Carrington; G. Marcy, SFSU/P. Butler, UC Berkeley/UK Schmidt Telescope/Skyview/Royal Observatory Edinburgh/Anglo-Australian Observatory/AURA; NASA/JPL-Caltech/T. Pyle (SSC)
18-19	NASA; NASA/JPL-Caltech/E. Churchwell, University of Wisconsin
20-21	NASA/ESA/G. Bacon (STScl); NASA/JPL; NASA; NASA; U.S. Mint; WORLD BOOK illustration by Matt Carrington; NASA/WORLD BOOK illustration by Matt Carrington; © David Watts, Dreamstime
22-23	ESO; NASA/JPL-Caltech
24-25	NASA/JPL-Caltech; NASA/University of Texas/NSF
26-27	NASA/JPL/PlanetQuest; Marty Harris/McDonald Observatory/University of Austin/Penn State Center for Exoplanets; WORLD BOOK illustration by Paul Perreault
28-29	NASA/JPL-Caltech/R. Hurt; WORLD BOOK illustration by Roberta Polfus; WORLD BOOK illustration by Roberta Polfus; NASA/JPL/PlanetQuest/The Lyot Project, American Museum of Natural History
30-31	WORLD BOOK illustration by Francis Lea; NASA/ESA/G. Bacon (STScl)
32-33	WORLD BOOK illustration by Bill and Judie Anderson; WORLD BOOK illustration by Roberta Polfus; AP Images
34-35	C. Marois et al/National Research Council Canada; NASA/ESA/G. Bacon (STScl); NASA/ESA/P. Kalas (University of California, Berkeley); NASA/ESA/L. Calcada (ESO for STScl)
36-37	© Mark Garlick, Alamy Images; WORLD BOOK illustration by Matt Carrington
38-39	David A. Aguilar, Harvard-Smithsonain Center For Astrophysics
40-41	NASA/JPL-Caltech; © Ron Miller
42-43	© David Hardy, Astroart; ESA/Alfred Vidal-Madjar, Institut d'Astrophysique de Paris, CNRS, France
44-45	NASA/JPL/Space Science Institute; NASA/Johns Hopkins University Applied Physics Laboratory/Southwest Research Institute; NASA/JPL
46-47	NASA/JPL-Caltech/T. Pyle (SSC); NASA/JPL/Space Science Institute; NASA/JPL-Caltech; NASA/JPL-Caltech; NASA/ESA/A. Schaller
48-49	NASA; © Ron Miller
50-51	NASA/Donald J. Lindler, Sigma Space Corporation/GSFC/EPOCh/DIXI Science Teams; © Shutterstock; WORLD BOOK illustration by Matt Carrington
52-53	University of Washington; © Susan Dabritz, SeaPics; © Science Source/Photo Researchers; NASA/NAI's Indiana-Princeton-Tennessee Astrobiology Initiative
54-55	ESA/C. Carreau; © Joshua Sosrosaputro, Dreamstime; ESA/Medialab
56-57	ESA/NASA/G. Tinetti, UCL; © Jarvis Gray, Shutterstock; © Shutterstock; NASA; © Shutterstock
58-59	ESA/D. Ducros, CNES; NASA/Kepler Mission/Jon Lomberg; Canadian Space Agency; NASA/Regina Mitchell-Ryall/Tom Farrar